Contents

INTRODUCTION

Even if you live in a tiny apartment, you should be able to grow some plants. In addition to typical houseplants, certain herbs, fruits, and vegetables can thrive in an apartment garden. Start with just a few containers as you hone your gardening skills. Factors, such as access to sunlight and the sheer weight of your containers, need to be taken into consideration. Here's how to start your apartment garden off right.

How To Grow Plants In Apartments

While some plants are more hardy and forgiving to beginner gardeners than others, all plants have specific growing needs that you must meet. Here are some elements to know as you're choosing plants to grow in your apartment garden:

- Sunlight: Most fruiting and flowering plants need a full day of sunshine. That means six to eight hours of direct sun. This can be hard to come by in an apartment especially in a city where tall buildings can block the sun for at least part of the day. Balconies and rooftops offer the best chance of full sun. If you're gardening on a windowsill, you can either choose plants that require less sunlight, such as certain salad greens and herbs, or you can add a grow light to mimic the sun's rays.

- Soil: Plants depend on their soil for water, air, and nutrients. Because your apartment garden will likely involve containers, you can't use ordinary garden soil. It will compact in pots, limiting air and preventing water from flowing through. Thus, a well-draining potting mix is necessary. Potting mix is light and fluffy, efficiently circulating air and water to keep roots healthy. And it's somewhat sterile, so you won't have to worry about bringing diseases into your apartment.

- Water: Plants in containers need a lot of water, often multiple times a day. So choose a spot for your garden that has easy access to a water supply. Carrying watering cans can get tedious, especially if you have several plants. If it works for your setup, consider purchasing a hose that can be attached to a sink faucet. It's handy when you need it, and it coils away when you don't.

- Humidity: If you are growing your plants on an indoor windowsill, you might need to provide some extra humidity, especially when the heat is on. Spritzing the plants with a fine mist can help, or you can place the plants near a tray of water.

- Wind: If your plants will be exposed to high winds, especially on a rooftop or from heavy traffic near a balcony, you might need some added protection. Wind can tear through leaves and overturn top-heavy pots. So provide a wind block, such as a screen or railing. Or make sure your containers are wide and heavy enough to anchor the plants.

- Weight: Containers full of soil are heavy to begin with, and once they are saturated with water their weight can triple. Make sure your apartment garden spot can handle the weight.

Window boxes will need to be secured to the windowsill. And if you're gardening on a balcony or rooftop, check with your landlord or building board about weight restrictions.

Best Plant Choices for Apartments

You can grow just about any plant in a container to a certain extent. For instance, a full-size apple tree might be out of the question, but there are skinny columnar varieties that can fit in a 1-square-foot corner of your balcony. Think about what you enjoy eating, and then choose a few types of plants to try out for your apartment garden. You can start with seeds, which offer more variety and are cheaper. But small nursery plants will get your garden established sooner.

- Herbs: Although many herbs grow well in containers, they won't get as large and bushy as they would outdoors in the ground. And you might have to replace your plants if you harvest frequently. But it is wonderful to have fresh herbs close by for cooking. Some top choices for apartment gardening include mint, chives, parsley, lavender, basil, and thyme.

- Salad greens: Salad favorites, such as lettuce, spinach, and arugula, are fast-growing, shallow-rooted plants. They're not overly fussy about their growing conditions, as long as they get plenty of water.

- Tomatoes: Tomato plants can get large and heavy, but they grow well in pots. They will do best in a container that is at least 30 inches in diameter, but you also can grow some of the patio varieties in a hanging basket.

- Chili peppers: If you like heat, hot peppers grow very well in pots, and they can set fruits year-round. You also can try growing sweet peppers in containers, but they typically don't do as well as hot peppers.

- Meyer lemons: Some of the easiest fruits to grow in a container are dwarf citrus trees. Meyer lemons do well indoors if they get six to eight hours of sun each day, along with some humidity. Put something underneath the pot to protect your floors and furniture, as lemon trees give off a sticky sap.

- Strawberries: A window box of strawberries is as beautiful as it is delicious. Strawberry plants generally need at least six hours of sun per day and consistently moist (but not soggy) soil to produce their best fruit.

There are certain tasks that you can expect to tend to regularly in your apartment garden, including:

- Watering: By far the most important gardening task is watering. Even if your garden is exposed to rain, that probably won't be enough water. The soil in containers dries out quickly, especially as your plant grows. Test the soil by poking your finger an inch or two below the surface. If it feels dry, you need to water.

- Feeding: You will need to feed your plants on a regular schedule, according to their individual growing requirements. A water-soluble fertilizer that can be added when you water is usually the easiest method. Also, note whether your potting mix has fertilizer already in it, as this typically will delay the need for you to feed your plants.

- Problems: Pests and diseases have a way of finding plants no matter where you grow them, and there are no natural predators for insects indoors. Inspect your plants for problems whenever you water them or harvest. If you spot signs of pests or diseases, such as discoloring or holes in the leaves, move that plant away from the other plants until the problem is remedied.

- Harvesting: Learn when your specific plants are at their peak for harvesting, and then don't delay picking the fruits of your labor. In some cases, harvesting actually promotes the plant to produce even more food for you to pick.

Apartments don't always offer vast amounts of space to indulge in gardening. But there's bound to be a sunny corner where you can test your green thumb and enjoy the fruits of your labor.

Every Tip, Tool and Trick to Get You Started on Apartment Gardening

'Tis the season when apartment gardening gets veerrry popular in thawing Madison. As Farmer's Markets begin anew and nurseries open their doors, apartment dwellers feel their thumbs going green. If you're ready to get started, we've compiled a listing of helpful tools, posts, videos and links to outstanding gardening blogs. Can you dig it?

GETTING STARTED GARDENING TOOLS

Before you buy a seed or pot a plant, you need the right tools to get the job done. Here's are the core essentials for any apartment gardener most of which you'll find for sale at gardening supply stores or online.

Garden Fork – Hand Cultivator – Ideal for loosening and aerating the soil.

- Gloves – A pair of washable, synthetic gloves should be fine for the urban gardener. Good for

deadheading, weeding and handling seeds. If
you're going to be doing bigger jobs, like picking
up leaves or dealing with thorny plants, get latex-
coated cotton gloves.

- Hand Trowel – A hand trowel is useful for
planting seeds, bulbs, etc. Opt for one with a
rubber handle.

- Hand Pruner/ Pruning Shears or Scissors – Used
for trimming, edging and cutting back plants.
Scissors work well for cutting twine and
removing dead flowers, while hand pruners are
best for small, woody plants or branches.

- Hand Rake – Useful for removing debris around
plants or picking up small piles of leaves.

- Watering Can – Watering cans come in a variety of shapes and sizes. Opt for one with measure marks.

- Mobile Planter – We'll detail some container gardening ideas further down, but the mobile planter allows you to move plants indoors and outdoors – ideal for Wisconsin winters

- Gardening Seat or kneeler/kneepads – You probably won't be using many long-handled tools, so kneeling and crouching will be the norm. These seats and kneelers go easy on the knees or bottom so you can garden in comfort.

- Tub Trug – Good for keeping tools together or collecting waste. You can never have too many containers.

Herb Drying Rack – Smart move for an herb gardner – a great way to dry out your herbs.

Helpful Apartment Gardening Posts to Get You Started

1. Getting Started with Container Gardening

Post Tools and Resources for the First Time Container Gardener includes some invaluable resources, and includes links to some techie garden items like the Koubachi Wi-Fi Plant Sensor (guide for monitoring soil moisture), self-watering containers, and modern countertop gardens.

2. How to Get Started with Herb Gardening

The Tasteful Garden includes a post or guide on Herb Gardening for Beginners. It must have a nice general overview on the process, along with links for more information on grow herb plants.

3. Starting your Own Organic Garden

For you budding (no pun intended) organic gardeners, check for information on overview for tools and materials; selecting seeds and planting; care and upkeep; and more. Includes a ton of links at the end for related organic gardening posts.

4. Getting Started on a Vegetable Garden

Check for some interesting thoughts on space usage – particularly apt for renters!

5. High-Tech Indoor Urban Gardening Tools

For the more advanced gardeners, checked for created post on a variety of high-tech tools for the more advanced indoor gardener that address growing methods, lighting systems, ventilation, and automation.

Apartment Gardening Guide

Growing your own food can be intimidating when you're drowning in a metropolitan sea of glass and concrete, but it doesn't have to be. Right now people are growing everything from chives and rosemary to lemons and tomatoes in their apartments, and you can too! You just have to get your hands a little dirty with this four step guide to urban farming.

Step 1: Location, location, location (and sunlight)

The number one rule in real estate also applies to the microcosm of your apartment: location. Location will dictate every other decision that you make in your new urban farm, so it's important to spend a little time thinking about it. Do you have a fire escape or balcony you plan on tilling, or are you trying to stay strictly indoors?

These are important questions to ask because they will decide which crops are available to you and where they should go based on sunlight requirements. In a city, it may be difficult to grow plants that require a full 6+ hours of light, because a lack of sun will lead to stunted growth or death. But don't worry Farmer, there are plenty of indoor and outdoor partial sun plants to be grown, and a whole array of of techni?ues to use.

Outdoor locations allow for more and larger plants, larger containers and usually more sunlight. However, this also leaves plants more exposed to the cold and pests, so depending on what you're growing you may need to bring it in before the first frost. That being said, you can take this chilly opportunity to plant flower bulbs that will stay dormant until spring, when they will spread their buds and thrive.

Indoor plants can still get enough sunlight, you just need to put them in the right place. Most plants you buy come with helpful guide explaining how much sunlight they prefer, and it's worth spending thirty seconds to read it. This will help you decide whether you should leave your herbs right next to the windowsill or in a nice, shady corner. But more on that later.

Step 2: Containers and pots and shoe organizers, oh my

Congratulations Farmer, you finished the first step! You decided on a few locations throughout your apartment, and are ready for the next step. Now you need to decide on potting, because real estate means nothing to your plants if they don't have a house to call home.

Unless you're growing something that needs an outrageous amount of water, drainage is a huge consideration. Much to my younger self, I accidently overwatered my venus fly trap when I was little, it turns out plants can drown. The best way to avoid this is making sure that your pot is prepared properly before planting anything in it.

Be sure you have enough drainage holes in the bottom, between half a dozen to a dozen half-inch holes should be more than enough. Many sites will tell you to put shards of broken pottery or gravel to allow for drainage, but this is only for pots without drainage holes. Finally, if you're planting inside be sure to have some sort of saucer under your pot, otherwise you'll have a very wet floor.

Speaking of potting plants, there's a whole host of different ways to do it.

For a more DIY approach, consider making your own pots out of old tin soup cans. They're cheap, easy and it's a good way to reuse and recycle just be aware that metal containers heat up much faster in the sunlight and can cook your roots.

Shoe organizers can be a great way answer to the question of vertical gardening in an apartment, just be sure to hang it on a stud in the wall, or else it could turn into a horizontal garden very quickly, with plants and dirt splattering on your floor. Similar to preparing a pot for planting, simply poke a few drainage holes in the bottom of the pockets. A rolled up towel inserted below the nail between the wall and the organizer helps keep the wall dry.

It's also possible with a drill, jigsaw and a few other tools, to make a self-watering pot, but that's a bit more advanced.

Step 3: Crops

Now for the fun part. What do you want to grow? This alone can be a daunting question, but there are a few factors to consider when trying to decide. What's your gradient of available sunlight? What plants do you like to use or eat? What makes the most financial sense to grow? What season are you planting in?

Personally, I grow almost exclusively herbs. Before, I'd buy rosemary or something for a recipe, end up using a quarter of it, and letting the rest go bad in my fridge. That's extremely wasteful, and it begins to get expensive. Now I just have to pick what I want directly off the plant.

However, available sunlight has the final say in what you're able to plant. Levels of sunlight are broken into four categories.

- Full sun (6+ hours of sunlight)
- Partial sun (4-5 hours of sunlight)
- Partial Shade (2-4 hours of sunlight)
- Shade (less than 1 hour of direct sun)

Carrots and green beans are more than happy in a partial shade environment, and there are a variety of dwarf fruit trees like kumquat and lime trees that can do well indoors. Beans, broccoli and scallions are also happy in a shady environment, just be sure that they get around three hours of sunlight a day.

With a little work, you can grow an entire salad in your studio apartment in Queens.

Step 4: Final Preparations

Here you go Farmer, last step! Preparations. There are just a few things you'll need to pull your garden together, all of which can be purchased at aforementioned hardware stores. Some of these may be optional depending on what you're growing.

- Potting soil- This is absolutely necessary! There are lots of different kinds of soil, dirt, and manure and it's not all considered equal. Ordinary garden soil can introduce disease and is too heavy for container plants, so it's necessary to get soil specifically for potting.

- Trowel- This is pretty important, as I've found soup spoons and ladles don't work nearly as well.

- Gloves- This is really up to you and your plants. I only use gloves when dealing with plants that have thorns, but to each his own.
- Garden Fork- Basically a mini pitchfork, it's really only needed when dealing with really compact, rocky or frozen soil, or when weeding.

- Fertilizer- This again is dependant on what's growing. Some plants require fertilizer once a month or so, others are perfectly happy without it. It's a case by case basis.

- Stakes & Twine- This is used when growing climbing plants like beans, tomatoes or ivy. It's important to stake them up for when plants get between half a foot and a foot tall to allow them to grow properly.

Gardening In An Apartment

If you feel you are losing out on the bliss of having a beautiful garden, to have created it, nurtured it, only because you are living in an apartment; then no need to feel disheartened about it. You can very well open your window and look at a beautiful garden outside or even have your own garden inside apartment.

Community garden

Community garden is the garden developed in the common area in an apartment complex to which every apartment dweller has an access. You can have a kitchen garden, terrace garden or a balcony garden in your flat, but to have a beautiful garden in the common shared area is a wonderful feeling that acts as a bond among all the apartment dwellers. You can grow flowering plants, vegetables, fruits or even trees there.

Community gardens may be supported by the apartment owners association/RWA in one locality or neighbourhood. It is a way of connecting with nature for those who do not have a balcony or enough space in their flats to create a garden. The garden can be a flower garden or a food garden with fruit plants and vegetables growing in the common area.

Flower garden:

In case of flower gardens the first thing is to know how to choose seasonal flowers in various seasons. The flowers you grow in the garden have to reflect the colour of the season – summer, spring, autumn and winter.

Spring blossoms:

Daffodils can be good choice for the spring seasons as the blossoming daffodils reflect the vibrant spring time.

Summer shines:

Garden roses – red and yellow match the sunny countenance of the garden. Along with them, rainbow of daisies, yellow dahlias and geraniums are the perfect matches for the summer time.

Autumn mellows:

Flowers bring to mind the picturesⁿue combination of chrysanthemums, hydrangeas, sunflowers and roses.

Winter greys:

The winter comes with its own dark beauty and the amaryllis fits best in the garden with the pink or red roses.

Watering a flower garden

The most common question that arises related to flower garden is how often should you water a plant? The right way to start off is how you should water a plant. Different plants need different amounts of water. As a general rule, flowering plants need about one inch of water a week. This includes any rain you might receive.

Plants with taproots need less water than plants with shallow roots. It depends upon the kind of soil you have your garden, too.

Plants in clay soils, whether shallow rooted or having a taproot, will need to be watered less frequently than plants in other types of soil. Plants in sandy soils will need to be watered more fre□uently and will need more water per week than plants in clay soils.

If you are putting the plants in containers, then you need to know that plants in containers need more fre□uent watering than ground plants. In case of plants in containers, allow the top 1 inch of soil to dry before watering, which means that you will need to water every other day or every second day.

Food garden:

Imagine yourself growing your own food in the area available in your apartment complex! It is not a wishful thinking but something that can be turned into reality with the help and cooperation of members living in the apartment. Your food garden may have both fruits and vegetables growing in it.

Vegetable garden:

You may go for a vegetable garden also. It is always a nice feeling that you have produced something at your own area. The vegetables will sprout, grow and ripened up. That too on the space shared by all of you!

Before deciding which vegetable to grow in your garden, you must remember that every region has its own specific climate and that the vegetables thrive in different seasons. Keeping these in mind, you have to choose the vegetables accordingly.

In the Indian climate, tomato, lettuce, broccoli, peas, peppers, spinach, chillies can be ideal for a community garden in an apartment. However, you have to keep in mind that adequate sunlight and watering is a must for the vegetables to grow.

You have the option of planting your vegetables in beds, pots or directly into the ground. You have to keep in mind that the soil must be well-balanced with a mixture of top soil and organic material such as compost, aged manure, etc.

You have to prepare your soil at least 3 weeks before planting time to give the garden area time to mellow.

Choose your veggies

Choose vegetables that are easy to grow and does not take up too many space. Let us take an overview of the vegetables grown in the garden that are proper for an apartment complex and the specific care they need.

Carrots are excellent as they can be grown small garden spaces. Salad carrots should be ready for picking within 10 weeks of planting and are good garden investment. However, they do not thrive in hot weather and must be cultivated during the cool season.

Herbs, such as parsley and chives, make excellent growing options alongside vegetables, especially lettuce. Lettuce is always preferred as they do not take up lot of spaces. Peppers take up very little space and they can look decorative when planted in small containers.

Tomatoes require sun shine and can be planted with plants, rather than seeds, to shorten production time. To grow tomatoes, planting should be in late spring time and you have to make sure that the soil is rich with organic matter.

Beets, cucumbers, eggplant, green beans, onions, peas and radishes are some of the other vegetables that are ideal in a small place.

Here are some guide lines to follow if you are going for a vegetables garden:

(i) Plan the design: The design has to be given top priority as it decides the ways in which the sun rays enter the garden and watering is carried out.

(ii) Do not clutter it with many plants: Too many plants will hamper the growth of vegetables. The bigger plants may shade the smaller plants, thus blocking the sun light.

(iii) Maximize the space: As apartments usually do not have a huge common area, you have to maximize the area available. One way to do it would be to grow vegetables vertically so that number of vegetables can be grown in a limited space.

Fruit Garden:

Fruit gardening is a novel idea for apartment gardens in India. Orchard fruits are the ideal plantation options for an apartment garden.

Apples, pears, plums, and peaches are the usual choices as they do not require annual planting. The trees that bear these fruits require pruning and maintenance and usually take 2-3 years before producing their first, modest crop.

However, you have to keep your limitations in mind. In a country like India, where climate varies to a large extent from Southern parts to the Northern states, from the dry mid-western parts to the perennially wet Northeast, it is not possible to have a coconut tree or an apple tree in every region.

Few fruits that can be easily grown in apartment gardens depending on the respective climate are – Blueberry, coconut, corn, watermelon, grapefruit, pineapple, guava, plum, mango, lemon, etc.

Things To Make Sure Before You Start Gardening

Before you start gardening, make sure to go through the lease agreement and there is no limitations to use the area you are intending to use for gardening. If you share the space with your neighbours, consult them before planting anything as they may have a different vision for the garden.

If you are starting a community garden, then you have to share costs and labor with the other members. If you plan to sell the vegetables or fruits, then the profit has to be borne with other members.

While every apartment community wishes to have a beautiful garden filled with flowers, it takes a lot utmost care and knowledge to create and maintain one. As most of the apartment dwellers are working professionals, they may not get the required time to plan and train themselves to create a garden. In that case, they can go with the option of vendors/housekeeping staff. The vendors are resourceful and expected to get the required seeds for the garden, maintain the garden, water the plants, make it sure that each flower/plant gets the required sunshine, etc.

Things to keep in mind while growing

- Tilling: Break the ground before starting any cultivation. Since it is a small plot of land, you may have to use pick, shovel and hoe to till the ground. This must be accomplished collectively. You should clear away any large stones, roots and limbs, heavy accumulation of vegetation, and other debris before tilling.

- Place the seeds: First step is to plant the seeds. You need to mark out the area where you want to plant. You can create rows with the help of a hoe or plow. You can also create a slightly raised bed in the loose soil in a narrow line, cutting across the plot. Then you'll need to place the seeds at the required depth in a groove.

- Watch out for insects: Insects find young plants more appetizing. So, in order to protect them, you may make use of surrounding bug repellent plants as a natural way. However, you may have to resort to insecticides to keep your flower and vegetable plants safe from the insecticides.

Organic Gardening

Organic gardening is nothing but growing fruits, vegetables and herbs in a natural manner, without the use of man-made chemicals and fertilisers. It is being widely favoured by more and more number of people now a days.

Ways to go for organic planning

1. Improve the quality of your soil to ensure healthy growth of plants. You can dig leaf mould and garden compost into the soil or spread them across the surface, so that rain, sunlight, insects and worms will help them get mixed with the soil. It will allow dry soil in your garden to soak moisture and nutrients.

2. Make your own compost. Every bio-degradable household waste – prunings, peelings, tea bags, old flower heads, bits of newspaper, etc can be turned into

nutrient-rich compost. You need to fill a compost bin with a good mixture of these compostable material.

3. Choose the right type of plants to grow in the garden. Survival of the fittest applies here and strong plants are less likely to succumb to diseases or pests. So, grow a plant that suits soil of your garden. You can also choose naturally disease resistant plant varieties that resists common insects.

4. Control weeds naturally. You can prevent weeds naturally by employing some common methods such as spreading compost or leaf mould across soil. As and when weeds appear, pull them up and pluck out the roots so that they cannot reproduce.

5. Control insects naturally. If you have pest problems you should use biological controls. There are many

natural solutions available like tiny parasitic wasps that can be used to control white fly in greenhouses and a microscopic worm that kills vine grubs.

6. Don't reach for a chemical spray when your plants come under attack. Instead make your garden a haven for animals, birds and insects and they'll control the harmful elements.

7. Make your garden a home for animals who can prevent unwanted species to thrive in your garden. For example, hedgehogs and toads prey on slugs and snails, while lacewings and ladybirds devour greenfly.

8. You can try out companion planting to save the plants from insects. Vegetables can be saved from pests if there is a scented plant nearby. For instance, French

marigolds planted near tomatoes can drive away the white fly.

Landscaping the garden

In colloquial conversations landscaping equates gardening. Landscaping is to transform the visible features of an area of land including the living elements such as flora and fauna. Although landscaping is the art and craft of growing plants in order to create a beautiful environment, other elements like structures, buildings, fences or other material objects created or installed by humans is also termed as landscaping.

With a little collective effort and vision, an apartment complex can have their own garden which they can boast of. The garden can be of various types depending upon the exterior of the apartment and the space and outdoor design.

- Path Lining: For apartment complexes that have paths between buildings, landscaping pebbles or gravel can be good option. To give it a polished, refined look, you may line the pathways with heavy embedded stones. The key thing is to put in kind of pebbles that would not be slippery when it rains as it would make it riskier especially for the kids. The pathways can be lined in gravel, matching the colour of the exterior of the apartment.

- Tired flower planters: If your apartment complex has large, open public areas, then tiered flower planters are the best ways to add visual impression. For it, you have to choose a wide base of bricks or stones that match the paving of the patio areas and install a planter with several levels. Thick walls and wide, flat tops can be placed to allow extra seating around the base. While planting flowers, they should be in the levels of the planter so they grow in lush groups.

- Trees: Trees add a homely feeling to the complex and render a neighbourhood touch. Prefer tall and sturdy trees are over delicate ones to keep the branches out of the resident's way and prune them so that the lowest branches are at least five- six feet above the ground. To keep the base neat, you can try out tiered flower planters.

Decorating your garden

You can give the garden a sophisticated look by so many ways. Apart from implanting decorative plants and trees, a garden can have innumerable decoration pieces ranging from bird feeders to fountains, gazebos, hanging baskets, etc. Here are some of the ways to decorate the garden space.

- Topiary: Most gardens follow the topiary style in order to decorate the space. The plants clipped to give many shapes and forms in the desired shape. Various trees, shrubs and other types of foliage are designed in a topiary way. The shapes can be of anything you fathom bears, peacocks, clouds, humans and others can be made in your garden.

- Bird baths: A garden can be rendered a look closer to nature. Chirping of birds amidst the shrubs, plants and trees in the garden is not unachievable. And one can easily find ways of attracting birds into the garden.

One of the best ways is to install a bird bath in your garden. Bird baths are made up of aluminium. They are available in various sizes and shapes with beautiful designs. Installing a bird bath welcomes colourful birds to quench their thirst, play and splash the water.

- Bird feeder: If your garden is large enough, you can install a bird feeder. Millets, sunflower seeds, safflower seeds, niger seeds, etc can be kept in the feeder so that the birds can come into the garden searching for food. Along with feeder, you can also set up a customized bird nest and the garden can be a home to birds.

- Pools and fountains: To build pool and fountain is one of the common decorative practices. A garden with a fountain or a spring can be one of the most decorative pieces. Different kinds of floating plants, flowers, fishes and colourful pebbles can be kept in the pool to give it a decorative look.

- Furniture and sculptures: You can build garden furniture using wood, plastic, aluminum, wrought iron and wick. The material used should ensure that the furniture are weather durable and water resistant.

Sculptures can be of anything — gods, human figures, animals, objects and others. The materials like marble, wood, bronze, limestone, granite and terracotta are used for these sculptures.

The Disadvantages Of Planting A Garden
Gardens require time and physical exertion.

Gardens can supply fresh food and improve the appearance of the landscape, but growing your own vegetables or flowers comes with some potential drawbacks. A backyard garden requires a great deal of work and commitment throughout the growing season. Acknowledging the disadvantages of growing a garden can help you determine if the project is worth the effort to you.

Time

A garden requires a time commitment from the planning stages through harvest time. The greatest investment of time is required when you first start your garden, but the work continues throughout the growing season. You'll need to weed, water and fertilize the plants. In vegetable gardens, you also have to harvest the food when it is mature. Sharing the work load with family members or creating a neighborhood garden can mean less of a time commitment for you.

Cost

Vegetable gardens are considered money savers, but a garden comes with its own expenses that may cost you more than buying the vegetables would. When you initially create your garden beds, potential costs include a tiller, shovel, rake, hoe and edging material. After the initial investment, the yearly costs are lower, but expenses still include seeds, plants, compost, topsoil, fertilizer, mulch and support systems like trellises or tomato cages. You also see an increase in your water bill for irrigation of the garden. Limiting your garden size can help keep costs under control.

Vacation Coverage

The typical growing season spans several months. In warmer climates, many plants grow most of the year. If you're gone for long periods of time, you'll either need to ask someone to watch your garden or risk unhealthy or dying plants when you return. Having a neighbor or friend harvest vegetables and perform garden maintenance tasks while you're gone can be repaid with fresh vegetables or cut flowers.

Lost Space

Even with efficient use of space, a garden takes away a portion of your lawn or patio. If your property is small, this means even less space for other activities like entertaining, playing or creating seating areas. Only making the garden large enough to grow what your family will eat can limit your lost area. Using trellises to train vine vegetables like peas or squash to grow vertically and mixing vegetable plants in with existing flower beds can also help.

Injuries

Gardening requires physical exertion, including lots of bending, stooping, digging and carrying. The repeated gardening actions put strain on your back and joints like your knees. If you already have problems with pain or limited mobility, taking care of your garden can worsen those symptoms. Lifting, stooping or performing other actions incorrectly may also lead to injury, such as a pulled muscle. I makes sense to keep your garden small if you have physical limitations and take breaks while gardening to avoid injury to your muscles or joints. You can also hire a professional to handle some of the garden care.

Benefits Of Indoor Gardening

There are many benefits to indoor gardening. More and more people are realizing that something is missing in their lives if they don't have plants in their environment. The truth is that many of us live in urban areas, in apartments and condos with no yards to garden in. Or our yards in many of the newer subdivisions are very small, with little space for gardens. But we are part of nature and need to have nature around us. So how can we accomplish this?

By having pockets of plants throughout our living environment. There are two kinds of indoor plants. The first are those that were meant to be houseplants and will live their entire life in your home. The second is a plant that is temporarily in your home but will eventually move outdoors. They share common benefits to you, as well as specific benefits unique to each type of plant.

1. EMOTIONAL WELLBEING

When you are confined to the indoors due to the weather, the season, or maybe because you work from home, it can increase your need for plants and flowers. That little spot of color helps to lift your spirits and make you feel happy. Put a pot of flowers in the window so when you look out at the drab winterscape, you have a cheery plant to remind you that spring will eventually return.

2. CLEAN AIR

Do you know that your house plants clean the air you breathe? Plants use carbon dioxide and give off oxygen. Some plants will even absorb some of the contaminants in the air. This is pretty important in our much more airtight homes. Aim for at least one plant in every room. Have fun with this part. Try different types of plants.

You will probably choose a few tried-and-true houseplants like pothos and a spider plant that are easy to maintain and pretty hard to kill. But try some unusual plants too. Maybe an orchid is a fun choice for you. They are available inexpensively and come in lots of colors. Or how about cactus or succulents? They come in all different shapes and sizes and can be grown in a regular pot or you could use a hanging pot.

3. COOKING

A great way to start indoor gardening is with an herb garden. If you love to cook, you can elevate any dish by using fresh herbs instead of dried. Include a pot of mint in your windowsill garden and add a sprig to your drinking water. Teach your kids how to pinch the leaves between their fingers for that rush of fresh scent. Add fresh basil to your pizza or spaghetti sauce. Upgrade the canned soup you're making for lunch by sprinkling some chopped chives on top or use them on your potatoes.

4. FLOWERING PLANTS

We all love flowering plants, and there are lots you can add to your indoor garden. In the winter, the first flowering plant that comes to mind is the poinsettia. They last a long time after the holidays and will continue to grow. They are now available in lots of colors and are even dyed to appeal to every indoor color scheme.

They will love being outdoors in the summer. It is much more difficult to get the repeat color, but it can be done. They need extended hours each day in the dark to get them to turn color; otherwise, you will have a very nice green plant.

Another popular holiday flowering plant is the amaryllis. This is a bulb that can be grown in soil or even just in water. The flower of the amaryllis is a showstopper, and it comes in many colors but primarily shades of red, pink, and white.

In the spring, you'll see lots of potted tulips, daffodils, and hyacinth. Hyacinths come with the added pleasure of filling the room with a beautiful scent. You also will find cyclamen and azaleas. If you have someone who likes to give you cut roses, ask for a miniature rose plant instead. It will spend the winter indoors, and then you can plant it outdoors in the spring.

5. ECONOMICAL

Start seeds inside. You can do this with a pot and some soil, but you will have a much better outcome if you spend the money on a seed starter kit. With a small investment in an indoor seed growing kit, you can start your own veggies and flowers to plant outside in spring. This is a great family project as well.

Plan what you want to plant and where. Set up an area in your home to grow in. Read the information on each seed package to determine when you need to start you seeds. You will need light. If you don't have a window or door with full sun exposure, you will have to hang a light fixture over your seedlings and be able to adjust the height of the light as the plants grow.

By starting your own vegetables, you can control the exposure your food has to chemicals found in pesticides and herbicides. You can go completely organic and chemical free, or just limit the amount you use to what you feel is acceptable. You plant what you will use.

If you want a small amount of kale to add to your soup, you won't be forced to buy a six-pack of kale and throw most of It away. You can purchase flowers in the color you want and the size you want them to be. Your kids will learn how plants grow and where our food comes from. And, all the seed starting supplies you purchased can be reused for years.

Adding plants to your indoor space will be a quick and easy way to increase your enjoyment of your home. If you do decide to start your seeds, you will extend that enjoyment to eating meals that include food you grew and cutting bouquets of flowers that you chose and grew also.

Garden Pest Control

"There is no gardening without humility. Nature is constantly sending even its oldest scholars to the bottom of the class." – Alfred Austin

You're so excited to start gardening, to grow your own food. You devise your perfect plan, assemble your new Tower Garden, plant your happy little seedlings, and enthusiastically tend to your plants as they grow. You do everything right, and your garden flourishes.

Then one day, you notice something is wrong. There are holes in your greens! You look a little closer and find a plump green caterpillar, gorging itself on your investment. We've all been there. It's a disappointing discovery.

But as Alfred Austin alludes to in the opening quote, gardening is just a shorter way to say, "trying to tame nature." And nature—by nature—is averse to taming. Even with the best intentions, we're all at the mercy of her wild ways, which sometimes include garden pests.

The good news is garden pests can be controlled without pesticides. In fact, with the right precautions, they can often be prevented. Read on to discover 3 natural ways you can fight bad bugs.

(Before you can effectively address a pest problem, you need to know what you're dealing with. Reference this list of 10 common garden pests for help with pest detection.)

Repel Garden Pests with Plants

Did you know some plants actually have pest-repelling properties? Growing such plants in your Tower Garden is one of the easiest ways to prevent pest problems (especially if you're growing indoors).

There are a number of plants that fall into this category. But when it comes to deciding what to grow, I'm a fan of maximizing value. In addition to repelling most pests, the following 4 plants also attract good bugs, offer health benefits, and taste great!

- Catnip prevents aphids, beetles, caterpillars and shield bugs.
- Dill prevents aphids, caterpillars, shield bugs and spider mites.
- Mint prevents aphids, beetles, caterpillars, shield bugs and whiteflies.
- Nasturtium prevents aphids, beetles, caterpillars and shield bugs.

In addition to these, other great plants to grow for pest control include;

- Basil
- Borage
- Chives
- Marigold
- Oregano

- Parsley

- Rosemary

- Rue

- Summer savory

- Thyme

Control Garden Pests with Good Bugs

Attracting natural predators is another simple solution to garden pests. And in my opinion, it's also the most interesting. When I found an assassin bug nymph, well, assassinating a pest on my tomato plant, my immediate response was, "I've got to take a picture of this!" Attract good bugs to your garden for natural pest control. OK, now that I've revealed my inner nerd, here is a most-wanted list of garden friendlies:

- Ladybugs and their larvae feed on aphids and other soft-bodied pests. Rejoice if you see these red-orange, spotted beetles in your garden.

- Lacewings and their larvae devour lots of bad bugs, including aphids, caterpillars, leafhoppers, scales, thrips, whiteflies and even insect eggs.

- Hoverflies resemble small bees (and they actually help with pollination!). Their green, slug-like larvae feed on aphids.

- Parasitic wasps are often almost too small to see. They prey on aphids and caterpillars.

- Predatory true bugs, which include spined soldier bugs, assassin bugs, pirate bugs and others, feed on various caterpillars and beetles.

- Spiders may not be what you love to see on your Tower Garden, but they're valuable allies, eating all kinds of pests. Plus, those that typically inhabit gardens aren't poisonous.

- Tachinid flies, which basically look like houseflies, are natural enemies of caterpillars, beetles and shield bugs.

So how do you get these good bugs in your garden? You can actually order them online and introduce them to your garden. But I'm a fan of attracting the good bugs naturally (which increases the likelihood of them sticking around, too).

The most common way to attract good bugs is to grow insectary plants, or pollen- and nectar-producing plants. As you might guess, this means growing flowers will certainly do the trick. But flowering herbs work, too. The following plants attract both pest predators and pollinators:

- Borage

- Cilantro

- Cosmos

- Dill

- Marigold

- Mint

- Rosemary

- Rue

- Thyme

Kill Garden Pests with Natural, Organic Sprays
Botanical sprays can actually harm good bugs. So consider these as a last resort. If you do use the following sprays, always be sure to:

- Apply them in the late evening, once the sun is low in the sky. Otherwise, your plants could get cooked. (I made this mistake once. Not pretty.)

- Spray plants liberally, taking care to wet the undersides of leaves. For these sprays to be effective, they must come into direct contact with pests.

- Use this natural spray formula to fight virtually all garden pests.

DIY Spray for Virtually All Pests

Credit for this formula goes to Rodale's Organic Life. It's effective for most garden pests and may even help deter rodents and deer. Plus, you likely already have the ingredients. Here's how to make it:

- Chop, grind or liquefy 1 garlic bulb and 1 small onion.

- Add 1 teaspoon of powdered cayenne pepper, 1 quart of water, and mix.

- Steep 1 hour, then strain through cheesecloth, and add 1 tablespoon of liquid dish soap (such as pure castile liquid soap not dishwashing detergent) to the strained liquid; mix well.

- To avoid skin and eye irritation, wear rubber gloves and keep the mixture away from your eyes and nose when preparing and applying it. Refrigerate any remaining spray for up to 1 week in a covered container.

Insecticidal Soap + Neem Oil Spray for Most Insects

This powerful combination is widely used among organic gardeners for aphids, mites, thrips, whiteflies and other small, soft-bodied insects. Hat tip to Future Growing, LLC for the following ratio:

- 1 tablespoon of insecticidal soap
- 1 tablespoon of neem oil
- 1 gallon of water
- After spraying, discard any remaining mixture and clean your applicator.

Bacillus Thuringiensis Spray for Caterpillars

Bacillus thuringiensis (Thuricide) is the "go-to" natural spray for caterpillars. You can pick some up online or in your local garden center. Mix and apply it according to the product label directions.

Tower Tip: If you shop for a pest control solution at a local garden center, keep in mind that organic-approved sprays will feature the OMRI seal of approval.

There are a few other natural sprays you can use. (If you're feeling adventurous, I've heard blending bad bugs with water makes a good preventive albeit slightly macabre—spray.) But I've personally used each of these and found them to be effective.

Other Ways to Control Garden Pests

I've outlined just a few ways you can effectively combat garden pests. But there are certainly others. Pheromone traps, traditional row cover cloth and sticky traps are also methods worth trying. Some solutions don't even re□uire any special e□uipment. For example, one of my favorite ways to remove aphids is by touching Scotch® tape to plant leaves. Pretty simple!

Light Calculation For Indoor Vegetable Gardens

It's important to calculate the amount of lighting needed for growing and indoor garden in an apartment. Once you have decided on your plant list, you will need to decide how to orient your grow lights and which kind of lights to buy. This is more difficult than it sounds, but in general, there is no such thing as too much light.

Fluorescent bulbs

If you plan on growing mostly leafy crops or root crops, you can get away with fluorescent lights on an adjustable chain. The biggest concern with fluorescent lighting is wattage per square foot.

For leafy greens, you want to aim for 40-50 watts per square foot of growing space. This means for a 5'x5' area, you will need 1,000-1,250 watts of output. However, most fluorescent bulbs only truly put out 1/3 of their stated wattage. For a 60w bulb, you can expect 20w to be available for plants.

Therefore, for a 5'x5' area, you want to aim more for 3,000-3,750 watts per the label. The more light you can direct down to the growing area, the less wattage you need. This is a large amount of light for a small area, and it's difficult to find these lightbulbs in hardware stores. Traditional fluorescent lightbulbs can work if they are changed regularly, and as long as the plants remain green and bushy, they are getting enough light. Use cool lightbulbs (above 3000k) for leafy greens and root crops.

LED fixtures

LEDs are the best grow lights. While fluorescent bulbs put out about 1/3 of the advertised output, LEDs are more efficient and can focus their output in one direction.

For flowering plants, LEDs are essential. Plants need blue light for leaf growth and red light to induce flowering. With LED fixtures, you can set them on blue while the plants are young, and switch over to red as they mature and begin to flower. This is difficult with fluorescent lightbulbs because they are either red (under 3000k) or blue (over 3000k) and changing the light color means changing out the bulbs.

Flowering plants need more wattage per square foot, so aim for 60 watts per square foot of growing space. Lights should be no more than 6" above the top of the plant to maximize light use.

While lighting for indoor gardening can be a complex calculation, it's also not exact. A system in a basement with no windows will need the full wattage per square foot from supplemental lighting. A system next to a well-lit window can thrive with less supplemental lighting due to natural sunlight. Overall, if plants look bushy and deep green, they have enough light. If they are long, leggy, and reaching, move the lights closer to the plants and add more lightbulbs.

Three Common Indoor Vegetable Garden Systems

Now that you've decided which plants you want to grow, and how many, it's time to design a system. We will cover the three basic setups, but you can customize them to fit your space and growing goals.

All systems

No matter which system you choose to build, there are some components that have to be implemented in all of them:

- Air movement – Make sure you have fans to circulate air around your plants.

- Fertilizer – Most indoor systems use a soilless, sterile media. Find a water-soluble fertilizer to provide nutrients.

- Consistent lighting – Plants need a dark period each night to utilize the energy they create during the day. This needs to be consistent. When day length changes, plants think the seasons are changing, and they may stop growing or begin bolting. Consider timers for consistent light times.

Containers

This is the simplest indoor growing method. You can use almost anything for a plant container, including old juice bottles, milk jugs, plastic totes, glass jars, and buckets. You can use soil for this method, or you can use a soilless growing media. Look for growing medias from raised bed garden suppliers.

Use larger containers for plants with complex root systems, and smaller containers for plants with shallow root systems. In general, the larger the plant, the larger the container. Make sure all containers have adequate drainage.

The difficulty with containers is catching the water that leaches through after watering. Obviously, you don't want this water draining onto your floor. Most recycled plant containers don't come with drip pans like terra cotta pots.

If you place containers on shelves, you can let the water from one shelf drip down onto the plants below. However, this can cause mold problems, and you will still need to catch runoff at some point.

The easiest way to do this is to put your containers on stands. They don't need to be tall; just enough to allow the water to drain. Put your containers on a table or shelf with a non-porous surface, and build a small lip around the edge to prevent dripping. You can either create a slight tilt to drain water into one location, or mop up the water with a towel.

You can also fashion makeshift drain pans for your containers and empty them each day. These give you more flexibility, but leaving the water will create pest problems, so make sure you empty them consistently.

Containers can be placed on shelves for vertical gardening spaces, or on tables to accommodate taller plants. It is difficult to support trailing plants in containers, so this system is best for leafy greens, root crops, herbs, tomatoes, and peppers.

Vertical window gardens

These systems are great because they maximize natural sunlight and minimize how much space you need to dedicate to your plants. However, they are tall and skinny, so it rules out large, bushy plants like tomatoes and peppers.

You can use PVC pipe and build a zig-zag structure like those marble toys, and drill holes in the top where you want to plant each plant. Then, as you water, the excess will travel down through the pipe and empty into a bucket at the bottom. This system works great for small, leafy greens, herbs, and strawberries.

You can also use a long, skinny container that fits in the windowsill and string twine up to the top of the windowsill to create a trellis. This setup works well for beans, peas, cucumbers, and a few miniature varieties of melons and squash. You will need to put this container on a small stand with drain pans underneath. Once the plants latch on to the twine, you can't pick up the container each day to drain the excess water from a drip pan. So, you need a permanent stand with movable pans.

You will still need supplemental lighting in this setup, but you can also harness the natural light by building a reflective wall to bounce sunlight back towards your plants. This greatly reduces the need for supplemental light, and may even support leafy greens and herbs by itself.

Hydroponics

If you want to grow large amounts of vegetables and fruits indoors, you need some sort of water-based growing system. The easiest system to build is a hydroponic system. If you want to have a source of protein on occasion, you can build an aquaponic system, which uses fish as the main source of nutrients.

A basic hydroponic system has a grow bed and a holding tank. Every 45 minutes, the holding tank pumps water through the grow bed and saturates the roots with nutrient-rich water. It holds water for 15 minutes, then drains back into the holding tank. Aerators keep the water full of dissolved oxygen.

You can use floating styrofoam mats in the grow bed to suspend plants in the water, or you can fill the grow bed with clay pebbles and plant them like you would in soil. You can also use PVC, drill holes in the top for plants, and pump water through a maze of piping.

Aquaponics is basically the same, but the holding tank needs to be able to support fish. The benefit of these systems is that you can grow much more per square foot than any other growing system (including traditional raised beds). You can also grow plants to maturity faster, meaning you can harvest more plants, more often, which means you can grow more of your food at home.

The downside to this system is that it's full of water. If the pumps stop working, your plants die. If there's a leak, you're looking at massive water damage. Water means algae blooms, so you have to become a layman chemist in order to maintain the nutrient levels properly.

However, these systems are easy to add on to and you can grow almost anything in them, except woody herbs. You can also put these systems in basements or garages, if you have enough supplemental light, and grow a substantial amount of food.

Consistent airflow is extremely important in water-based growing systems, so make sure you have fans running constantly.

Building a hydroponic system is beyond the scope of this article, but there are many DIY kits available, and with a little construction knowledge, you can customize your own system for fairly cheap. The best materials for these systems are recycled 55-gallon drums, IBC totes, and plastic bins.

Conclusion

Growing your own food is a fun adventure, and it opens up the possibility of growing new and unique vegetable varieties. As you begin growing indoors, you can work towards building a self-sufficiency garden that provides fresh, healthy vegetables year-round.

A new generation of urban gardeners has emerged. From low-maintenance succulents to full-on vegetable harvests, apartment gardening has never been more popular. And for a good reason. Renters and beginner gardeners alike, Apartment List is here to help. Below is a list of tips and tricks for starting your apartment gardening journey.

Succulents

1. Start Small with Succulents

Start small and choose your first plants carefully based on ease of care. Succulents make terrific first plants for beginners as they are virtually maintenance-free and come in a myriad of varieties such as jade, aloe vera, zebra plant, panda plant, and echeveria.

Desk plant

2. Consider Your Schedule

Pick plants to grow based on the amount of time you have to devote to your fledgling garden. Low maintenance types for those with a busy work schedule and fast-paced social life are best. For those homebodies and work at home freelancers, growing high maintenance species will be challenging but highly rewarding.

Room Natural light

3. Think About Your Apartment Layout

Choose your first plants based on the positioning of windows and amount of light available in your space.

Apartment garden varieties that thrive in the interior recesses require minimal light while some demand direct sunlight for hours a day.

Weeping figs

4. No Windows, No Problem

For apartments with minimal windows, choose plants that are happiest in low light areas such as weeping figs, peace lilies, ivy, money plants, and fittonias.

Cactus absorbing light

5. Make Use of Your Light

Lucky apartment owners who have multiple windows with ample hours of full direct sunlight will be able to grow a wide variety of house plants such as cacti, succulents, and tropical flowers.

Fresh vegetables

6. Step Up Your Cooking Game

Home chefs and health-centric apartment dwellers will love tending to and harvesting from an indoor kitchen garden. From artisanal lettuce to mini tomatoes, there are practically endless tasty plants to grow.

Don't forget to spruce up those meals with some herbs! A kitchen window provides ample space for creating a small herbs garden with favorite flavors to jazz up your dishes.

Flowers

7. Brighten Things Up with Flowers

For those who love flowers, annuals such as pansies, geraniums, petunias, and begonias will provide beautiful blooms.

Hanging plants

8. Think Vertical

For small apartments and studios, vertical planters that attach to the walls will allow you space to grow. Choosing slim and tall potted plant varieties will free up space as well.

Plants on window ledges

9. Utilize Your Window Ledges

Window ledges can be used to hold long rectangular planters and tiny pots for a window garden effect. Be sure to choose plants that will thrive in full sunlight and make sure to turn plants, so they don't grow against the glass in the direction of the sunlight.

Miniature Trees

10. Freshen the Air

Plants can purify the air, so placing them in the most oft-used rooms of the apartment can provide the most health benefits.

Macrame hanging plant

11. Play with Macramé

Hanging plants in fun macramé planters allow you to garden in even the tiniest spaces. Ivy and other vines will provide an eye-catching aesthetic when cascading down the sides of the planter.

Colorful planter

12. Add Splashes of Color

Add pops of playful color with vibrant-hued planters in a variety of shapes and textures. Mix and match for an energetic display you and your plants will love.

Uni□ue planter

13. Be Creative With Planters

There is no end to the creative and uni□ue planters available, a throw-back favorite has always been the Chia Pet and there are loads of other playful planters available instore and online.

Watering pot

14. Stick to a Watering Regimen

No matter the plants you choose to get started gardening indoors, it's imperative you follow a watering schedule based on each plant's needs. Many people water their plants on the same schedule, which can lead to overwatering. Each plant has uni□ue needs and water requirements.

Packing soil

15. Use your Resources

Consult with the care instructions provided if you buy full-grown or starter plants. Additionally, the internet provides a plethora of valuable information for the care of plants based on species.

Plant soil

16. Don't Disregard the Soil

Soil type is important for plant health and growth. Many plants prefer a higher acidic to neutral soil with 7.0 pH level or above. Fertilizer can be used in potted plants but should be mixed with regular potting soil to avoid over-fertilization. Make sure all planters have enough drainage provided by holes in the bottom. A single layer of rocks can be added to the bottom of the planter to avoid blockage of drainage due to compacted soil.

Gardening tools

17. Invest in Modern Tools

Today's expansive and exciting range of modern gardening tools, accessories, and accouterments has never made gardening for beginners easier. You can discover everything available to get started with your apartment garden just by searching google or amazon.

Mini greenhouse

18. Consider the Humidity

Mini greenhouses and portable greenhouse covers are helpful for an apartment with a low humidity environment. Some varieties of plants grow better in high to medium humidity conditions such as dracaena, begonias, and ferns.